AF324763

Ralph J. Mills, Jr.

EACH BRANCH

EACH BRANCH

POEMS 1976-1985

Ralph J. Mills, Jr.

SPOON RIVER POETRY PRESS

1986

This book is published in part with funds provided by the Illinois Arts Council, a state organization, and by the National Endowment for the Arts. Our thanks.

Published by Spoon River Poetry Press, David Pichaske, editor, P.O. Box 1443, Peoria, Illinois 61655.
Dust jacket by Mary Martin, Sterling, Illinois.
Typesetting by Rodine the Printer, Peoria, Illinois.
Printed by M & D Printing, Henry, Illinois.

ISBN 0-933180-89-6

CONTENTS

for Helen, Natalie,
Julian & Brett

A Blessing

The dream last night—
my father was cleaning a fish:
the head cut off
neatly, guts
removed,
then the scales showering down,
tiny silver coins
flying ahead of the knife.

I watched, standing aside,
who had been fearful
to do the task.

And you, dead so long,
returned to calm my sleep,
a blessing
in your gestures.

I

from

WITH NO ANSWER

Days to Come

Thinking of what days are to come,
I see sun-ripened firs,
beds of fallen needles,
and listen to how the wind invades
their branches, seething,
how the sky comes down on them
bearing its freight of snow.
When I walk out,
roads and streets keep a secret,
the kind of meaning they won't give up.
Each day's like a hand extended—
I take it while it's there,
remembering that one
must be an empty glove dropped in the grass.

A Walk

> —for Robert Bufalini

I know where to look—
you wait beneath
summer trees, the leaves
swelling on a wind
twenty years old.

After dark, a walk
in silence—
we hear insects whirr
and music
from sun porch windows,
see church lit
for evening confessions,
each house in place.

A night light wavers
in the grocery
over melons, grapes,
sleeping flies,
our glancing faces stained
incandescent blue.

Freights whistle distantly
beyond us
down the Milwaukee line;
a last vacant
commuter rumbles north.

From the crossing,
rails narrow past sight—
rain or full moon,
they run out, taut
and glinting, ways we
pointed, wanting to go
once—and did.

The Way

I

Summer's dried husk
peeled and fallen—

The narrow channel waters
lie glazed,
straight and silvery as a pin
let drop between
scarlet, rust
or brown faded bushes.

Nothing but sunlight moving
inch by inch,
and a single flat cloud
wing feather
cirrus
frayed along its trailing edges
climbs
on the high westerlies
long and slow.

II

Windless air rests against
branches, grass,
the weedflowers
still white and yellow.

You point to
a street of vacant houses,
telling how
as the sky
darkens in their windows
you'll step
into shadow and haze
gathering up the trunks of
tall elms, with
a thin cold rain starting
to descend—

You speak of this as more
than a friend,
as one who will lead
the way.

5

Mid-August

I

Another night at 4 a.m.,
heavy, thunderous in the heat,
masses of cloud
shouldering each other—

the sky's
black basin cracks across;
marbled
with lightning.

Branches of cherry and elm,
the tree of heaven clash,
subside,
       begin again,
threshed out in a blur of
streetlights, of rain
that whipsnakes
in the air over pavements.

II

And the house in darkness,
everyone asleep.
Breath, hum of
fan, air conditioners;
a single lamp burns along a hall.

I sit up to listen,
thinking of
the weight of each drop,
how pools fill up, grasses
are beaten flat
and the wind lunges brokenly.

6

III

Day reassembles: the sun
reddening old bricks of a wall
etches shadows—this lacework
of leaves—precise
in tips, curves, serrated
edges, as a draughtsman would
have them—
          your shadow and mine
there too, morning's coolness
grown perceptibly sharper among
altering gradations of shade.

Poem

> "The sky's blue varnish . . ."
> —Anna Akhmatova

The sky's blue varnish gleams.
A bench in the grass
where elms, maples stand rooted
among their shadows
with afternoon sun sifting through leaves—
only a few have fallen.

Hands calm on the wood's warmth,
my thoughts nowhere else.
Here this moment
is what it seems,
and the clock of September
winds down.

Someone Might Say

Grey: grey and
predictable
the November twilight
washing out—

       Held there
rain-splashed, darkly
gleaming,
spiked twigs, branches of
cherry, ash
and a locust too
its pods curled like commas—

they shudder
tense against a northwest wind's
icy flail

      A season
"to go over things" as someone
might say—
window frames hammered by gusts
a high persistent
whistle
or hum of air, of voices
come close

tuned up
and working in edgewise

Horse

(After a poem by Jules Supervielle)

This sea, its sound incessantly
with us—even trees tossing wild plumage
know it:
        but the black horse
plunged in up to his flanks,
the long arc of his neck bent as he
nibbles the water's sweetness,
would trade the hot sand beach
and flat pasture
for breakers crested with foam
like the white backs of sheep,
for depths where he could feed
on sea grasses, gallop
hidden valleys and plains in a green
shimmering,
and leave behind him
traces of legend.

Yet he must wait,
pledge himself over each day,
gazing
at wave and spume, the sun-dazzled,
starlit wash of sea
that rises, falls away,
dreaming of a death
to come
while he shakes out his mane,
lowers his head to snap off the stalks
in a baked, dusty field.

Variation on Apollinaire

> —for Isabella Gardner

Only a girl
who watches a rider
crossing distant fields
and dreams of the past
of a ship he commands
entering history or legend
foam curling white at the prow
harsh winds shifting
while light bleaches the canvas
then Mytilene
blue harbor of Lesbos

These two
hold between them now
a flower
a single rose scrolled
petalled with fire
that breaks from their eyes

What sun having lost
its way still can scatter clouds
refuses to move on
but draws closer
and closer
to those expectant
dreaming lips
parted in their first smile

Postcard With a Painting

—in memory of Glen O'Malley

I

Oak, silver maple and willow—
stripped clean
they stand along the edge
of an iced-over lake
someplace
where the midwinter sun fiercely
resists dying
and heaves flame
above a line of smudged trees
and snowbound hills.

II

Skaters, walkers, a pair of
ice fishermen
track paths across this pond,
careless of wind
that's ready to sever bone
from bone.

I can see their eyes
rimmed with cold, the scarlet cheeks,
and breath curling past lips
as everyone hurries
through the descending night,

voices, thinned by distance,
carrying
far over the blackened shore.

III

In the painting there's only
one house,
which hunches beneath
tall elms, its windows
unlit, snow heaped
around the walls.

I reach a door, hidden
by drifts—

IV

This side of the picture
is perfectly empty—
     no tree
or footprint, not the stars'
shivered glass, nor any dark
overhead—
    a white
card without message,
whiter than
fields or frozen lake,

or the air
which has started to fill
with snow.

Only

In this dark, still room,
which is only a thought,

your star rises again
over calm water,

the air placid in blackness
as it drifts

always farther,
remote and luminous,

no more a face or body,
nor a wing left to shadow me—

only a name, which is mine,
and a receding light

in the room, across the water
wherever it is I lie down.

I

The lake swells, restless at dawn:
presses, drops back,
lifts again, slides, deep green
and frigid
under layers of ice
bedding it down.

Thoughts rise in the first
hesitant light,
then bare themselves familiarly—
loose, ragged, they begin
to dance, prodding
with a dull blade.

II

Yesterday on this branch of
winter-stripped maple
a cardinal sang, intent—
with no answer.

I watched the red shape of him
high up, listened
to his call stretch out an afternoon,
blue

and more blue still
against dusk's solvent edge.

15

Midsummer Rain

Days of midsummer rain—
earth dark, sodden with
pools of water and leaves,
the dirt churned
to thick wet clods.

Aimless of work, of thought,
staring at rain
that sways on an east wind's
slightest push—
                silvery grey
in fold and billow, tall curtains
flung loose—
                I have come
at last
into the dusk-lit room.

Night Song (I)

Hours past midnight
cool wind
lifts the curtains
lazily blowing

Blue as gas flame
the sky
around the moon's nimbus
a pearl radiance
spread
in ring after ring

What moves in the street

Moonlight, leaf
shadows
flocking together
beneath linden and maple—

careless they dance

Late Moon

                    —for Stephen Berg

                    I

Thin, wasting,
a late moon curves down
its arms—

This bone fragile, bone white
embrace
is enough to bring tears.

                    II

I reach a hand
deep into leaves of maple,
moonlit and
glossy black.

To enter
and be air: a draft
among branches,
wrinkling grass, weeds, shifting
a shadow or two—

then dropping flat,
motionless
on calm lake water.

                    III

What is it?
Hand, arm, loving eye,
an uplift of wing—

but tugged,
tugged back from the moon's arc,
the walls, cliffs,
domes of night cloud
high and dark to the west.

Some Kind of Voice

> —for Al Poulin

I

Some kind of voice
blurred like a restless sleeper's
breath—
        I listen
to the locust branches
wind stirring
through, under them
the sky overhead
threaded with cirrus
                        as westerly
a grey smear of rain
thickening the horizon
begins to move in

II

The kitchen table's white oval
is smooth as an egg
                        or tear—
all around
yellow walls and ceiling flatten
into one sun-splashed field
where painted flowers
grow expansive

                        I want to
survive like them
if only a while—
                        with an ear
for the rain's syllables:

an insistent beat
then light music
diminishing
            —so delicate—
from leaf to branch, from tree
to grasses to the dark
ground inward

19

II

from
MARCH LIGHT

A Stalled Spring

A stalled spring:
April is
done with
          and the trees
scarcely in
leaf
          their highest
branches whitened
by cold glossy
sunlight
          or shimmering
now
from a patchwork of
mist, drizzle
the small steady
falling—

          Struck panes
run with it, down
in rivulets:
                    roof
tiles, this window
go dark
beneath
          as air stirs
the day's
grey scenery

Two in June

> —for Michael Anania

       I

A dawn
wind keeps shaking
the maples
       sticks there
trying to
pry loose—

       And the leaves
let it go

       "Sibilations"
you might have
said: this whispered
breathing
       of day

       II

Then the clouds'
splendor:
       large & puffed
bordered with
orange
       changelessly
changing
       luminous or dark

"Purpose"
       speaking only
for myself
       "to be
moving with purpose"

7/6

The sun's brassy
glare
        on metal & glass—
even concrete
                gives out a hard
white light
                though muted a little
by the wet air
                today
                so furred & heat-
burdened
                each step's in
slow motion—

                A life
narrowed down
                not to ritual but
some kind of round
                then broken
occasionally:
                say, by this morning glory
throat open & tilting
                up through
iron railings
                of a church fence—

Or driving north:
                masses of blue flowers
above a ditch
                purple bull-thistles, thick bunchy
weeds
                by the road's shoulder
wavering in the slightest wind
                                & past them
from a rise:
                fields in view, with their
green corn shine

Beeches

This day, so hazy
and blinding
windless in July's wet heat—

Wasps, their long bronze bodies
hovering in sunlight
prowl the ivy
where it climbs a brickwork wall
and lie pulsing
on ledges

Coppery
or blackish purple
the rough leaves of beeches have swollen
to a cloud—
              its indolent
shadow printing
the grass
leans gradually toward me

Summer Nights

I

The afternoon greys a shade
each hour,
                lines of rain
edging north.

An air that's warm, burdened,
sleep heavy—
                small winds
push through the ash leaves,
the maples,
                a few already
rust brown in June.

                At the window
I wait for dark.

II

                Thirty years since
on summer nights at my grandparents'
with lamps off
for coolness,
                we ate or talked.
Aging elms
stirred overhead, scraping
the porch roof.

When the heat broke into
storms,
                trees keeled, rose again
like waves far at sea.

I stood looking
                and felt my arms
inside the branches
                sweeping down
and across
rain-drenched grass.

27

On a Wind

> I

A neighboring
bird cherry tree
lively
     with sparrows
almost reaches
this top floor
window

     Above the
grass
   a shadow-mime
at first light—
       leaves of
red maple
     playing
before a white-
washed wall

> II

July days
spending again—
      the heat
builds slowly
     dampness
blurred to mist

Out walking
    I watch a
ribbed and
feathered
     longstemmed cirrus
it floats
past branches, leaf
thickets
    on a wind
urged eastward

III

A room, a small
cave
        the breeze enters—
shades flap
snapping at wire screens
and glass

            This chair
faces west
toward the dusk
                    broken
flame-dyed
sky, greying roofs—

        below them
wild violets and white flowering
chickweed
            nod into
the hot dark

Fragrant Forest

    (Variation on Max Ernst)

The moon's iron ring
has caught
among stiff branches
bare of leaves

Here the gate of night
unlocks those
hidden glades
the pallid moon
can't touch

Water stirs, streams
wind beneath giant trunks
rivers are whispering
through buried roots
thick as lovers'
tangled thighs

Perfume of musk
of black loam
lifts in waves
toward the midnight sky
breath of a sleeper
haunting the forest
like a beast after prey

Somewhere above
stars could be hanging
jeweled eyes
but they're not to be seen
and the hand with its brush
has just stopped

For Bob Schuler

     A baby
hawk/
   up
over the dirt track,
     this old
bulldozed rail
bed,
   shrub, ditches of
stiff green reeds
     & ''lilywort,
look'' John said
      his shoe
in the ooze—

     Feather &
tendon,
    wings stretched
in a glide/
    the Red
Cedar steady
     below
with its tufted
islands—

    Hand pointed to
round hills
nearby,
    leafless trees
black with rackety
crows—
    but here's
where the scroll un-
rolls/
   words
out among birch &
white pine

Yellow

I

Over against the dense green
leafage
of a locust tree
its yellow and blackspotted
scrolled pods
shaking
      the grey tide of clouds
running high, heads
southeastward
         broken now
and now again
by a bright spill of sunlight

II

Autumn:
the haze before dark,
air damp
as in August, still untouched
by cold—
      but the trees
going brown, golden yellow or rust
erect above
their shadows, their first leaves
fallen to the grass

And the year drifts
—what
could hold it—
        slips in the current
loose between fingers

this flow with
no moorings

III

A perfect half
of moon
when the sky clears

above roofs and the blue-
veined phosphorus
light of expressways

On my windowsill
one tiny
yellow flower
unexpectedly blooms from the
dark tangle
of an aging primrose

A Fall Song

> —for R. S.

The cherry tree
crown's
          gone bare—

and sycamore
                    maple
ash, then elm—

               with leaves
in places ankle deep
& stuck
             wet
to my shoe

             Soon, soon
a first snow
                  ice-
luminous in the
thick half-light
                    of afternoon
when the roads start to
close—

Two Poems

       I

After chill fall
showers
      ivy climbing the
dulled rust
of old brick
        gleams
green as bottle glass—

And over chimneys, roof-
peaks
      huge blue &
sun-flushed
cumulus
      in procession
through a depth-
less clarity
       the air's own
while the wind
grips
    aimed along
a line from true north

       II

Lights come on
in the trees—
      it's willow
      & the honey locust
yellow against
evening
     small fires
lit in this pocket
of dark
    I stare into

thinking how a leaf be
tween leaves
     loosens
at the stem—
     in its veins &
     far off
the only message is
      snow

I

Not sudden dusk
                but a
late lingering sun
floods the ivy
                each leaf
face to the light

                its shadow
risen behind
        & painted black on the
pink brick
                the cloud-grey stone

II

No white clover
                little yar-
row or
        thistle's purple
left
in these empty lots
                nothing

    but a few
tasseled weeds & ghosts
of weeds
                spindly
bent twigs
                rooted under
& stubborn

III

      I stay out walking
while a hard wind
          crowds into
the elms—

       they buck &
  break up
in a rough surf of leaves
double-
toothed
      sawing the air

IV

Looking at old photo-
graphs today
        my face, yours
I almost didn't
know—
      the trees emptying
around me
      I stared through
clear to the bone

Night Song (II)

I

Pale underleaves of
the white ash
ruffled by wind at dusk

A blackbird, cawing
flaps across the park

Far up
what light is left
greys, fades out
trailing a stripe or two
of purplish cloud
down the skyline

II

The moon a rind
stars gathered into wheels, rivers

or isolate atoms
flickering in the gulf

I rub the toothed edge
of a leaf
            and turning
wonder if I'm at an age when
I want to live
only in the past

Dry flakes of moonlight
sift
through the trees
                        unexpectedly
cold on my skin
as a first bite of November snow

On a Birthday

Surfacing with the corner
ash tree
the sycamores, evergreens
into wet dawn light—

After three days
the wind has dropped,
a yellowed bone button of
December moon
hangs west, growing faint.

Rows of disheveled maples,
branches stiff with cold—
then near the park
                        weedstalks
motionless and brown
lifted
from snow patches
                        where sparrows
pigeons glide down
to scavenge
among wind-flattened grasses
and grey fingers of ice.

Forty-seven years—
a scattering of clouds high up
moves on
through an almost colorless
morning sky.

Four in December

I

December's fine-
grained
dry snow
pelts hard
across thick beds of
leaf and
withered grass

II

Red ash
       red
ash
beyond the window
polished limbs
quivering

III

Raggedy
sycamores too
in a
place I've walked
by
    some
still bearing
their rough furred
fruits
     with one un-
stripped maple
that rasps
chatters
to any wind

40

IV

Early light
          a sky
opening into rifts of
blue
        there
a thinned moon
tilts
pebble-white
in its diminishing
                  and I
grow motionless
leaning out from my
shadow
on the sill

No Moon

No moon
            not
one thin
rib of its hulk
left afloat—

            but there's a
black window
with stars
            an ash
tree shrugging off
air

    & somewhere the dead
in fading gowns
                who
even now
            wait to be
dreamed of

From this window
the cold reaches of sky westward
swarm
with fierce roseate clouds

A year's wheel
has creaked round to beginnings
through rutted ice
                    uphill
into the wind's frigid maw

Smoke feathering above roofs
silver against
                    mauve
and delicate blue of the air
before dark

Recognizable in my dream
the January field
                    you crossed once
your black hobbled wing
traces of its shadow moving over snow

Winters

I

All night
I thought thousands of
cold, bleached moths—
unseeing, suicidal—
dove below the streetlamps.

I leaned over the window
ledge—
a narrow arm of snow
stretched there
and along each black branch.

Breaths rose
out of dead grass, the heaped drifts:
a cloud
hid my face
as if it were the moon's.

II

From a train
delayed among winter fields
in the Dakota night
my compartment window dropped
its rectangle of light
shadowless
on the flat snow.

I stared hard
at that unbroken whiteness—
far ahead
like a tethered animal
the engine was tugging and hissing steam
into the dark.

44

Amherst Songs

> —for my sister, Anne Laurie

I

High clouds are combed thin
over Amherst way
            the sky's
wintery blue suffused with
sunlight
         glazing ice on the Connecticut River
that snake-winds its valley
& shines

II

Down Main &
away from town
          firs, thick-waisted maples
the air
greying around them
at day's close
        Wind sways
          only through
trees in front of
Miss Emily's homestead

Across the street
        I pick up & pocket
this small cone
from a larch
       for luck

45

Near Four

Near four,
stirred from a dream I can't keep
or reach back to,
I find an early February moon,
rags of smoke, chimney plumes
adrift on its face.

The lake stretches east,
a field of broken ice, slabbed and cobbled.
No clouds,
no shapes forming, altering
as in sleep,
only blueblack sky
and a nimbus of blurred silver.

At seventy, my mother says:
"How strange. Nothing changes inside—
you *feel* the same."

I look down a thread of moonlit street
drawing its length under trees—

                    they're maples
whose tatter of brown leaves,
brittle, tinny,
grips winter long, beating out
sharp, infectious tunes
to the wind, the blown snow.

In-Between

                    I

Almost evening—
the northern sky
            iron & violet
broken cloud off the plains
blown east
                    wind
pitching the trees
                    with now
& then again
                    a quick grate of
                    sleet—

                    II

At the shore-
line
        lake gulls scatter
        wide
& white as a
snow squall
                    falling suddenly
above the grey-
green chop of waves
                            they fish
a break-
water's tip

                    III

                    And
out of hard ground
        in-
between
            chips, splinters
of ice:
            pallid
blades & the frail
wavering strands—
                        these
                    grasses standing

Brief Thaw

I

Winter grasses,
pale brown
and leveled under snow,
the black forks of
twigs prodding for air.

In today's sunlight
a brief thaw—
the sky arches,
flares wide, streaked
with cirrus.

II

Snow loosening
like shale
slips down the roof gables.

I'm drawn toward
the water pooled at curbs:
thin rivulets running off,
bits of ice
carried away—

Vein, bone, body
all afternoon in a light trance,
a haze,
moving to a high-pitched music,
the bell call
of seeping drains.

Gone

Rain sluices the choked gutters:
winter's trash
flaked with soot,
last month's snow spilling away.

Bare-limbed,
a maple leans its tough, spidery branches
into March wind.

Fifteen years gone
among roots and thawing grasses—
at the mirror this morning
I startled your face
staring into mine.

March Light

Into grey March light,
and air
barely stirring,
these skinny, twigged branches
of an ash
tug up
resolute, unbroken
by winter storms.

You look out at the shapeless
pillowing clouds,
a rainslick street below,
familiar
as this room where
you've turned around,
and again
round,
to arrive without ever leaving,
never to arrive.

But with dusk,
seeing grasses blacken
the years of wind have humbled,
you long
to wade among them,
plunging down suddenly,
wordlessly—
ankle, knee and elbow—

as into deep water
or beneath a covering wing.

In Michigan

I

Crows squabbling
through faint rain
            a mist
in the leaves—

            black-
backed shine of
wet asphalt
                enters
the crowded trees

II

Roadside
by the woods' edge—

my daughter
finds there, in drab
twilight
            a glimmer
of bunchberry:
                    minute
white flowers clustered
                balancing on
long stems, tough
to break off

III

Clouds slip southeast
leave a paper-
thin shaving
                    all of the
moon there is—

but still lustrous
silvery
                the lake too
which a quick wind
frets
            pressing tall
reeds in the water
to restless
                    night-long talk

Three Pieces

I

A third day of
gales:
          the wind
hitting forty
or more
               bird cherry & maple
               nubs of plum
sprouting in April's
quick heat
               the dry air: dust-
laden, swimming with
grit
          clouds piled
southwest
               just before
a storm—

II

The ground lies
          rain-damp
around walls—
               but though
there's no hare-
bell here
               blue-eyed grass
has sprung thick
                    in a narrow
side garden
               mixing with
broken stone
brick
     in among or
under the bushes' wiry
coils
     & barbed twigs

III

Easter moon
            hung up
lustrous
            through the
undulant smoky cloud-
tides
            crossing its face

How "sadly we
discover
            what we are—"

            Yet
these new leaves—
            silver & black
& of a
lunar cast—
            the air
            so much calmer now
testing them gently

Porch Steps

                    I

This yard's one
plum tree
                    flowers in red
the spear-
tipped leaves
                    of deepest green—
or so they
seem in falling
dusk
          clarity of sky
a wood fence
dense warming air
                              close around

                    II

Day
          drawn to
conclusion
                    a little sun
burning an orange
fringe
                    on the clouds
far up
                    and soon
the stars flicker
in place, a moon's half-
lidded gaze
                              drops
among branches of ash
their lean shadows
                                        woven crazily
over the ground

III

       Standing
on porch steps
        my feet
rise out of
shadow
     my own kind
of craziness
the moon can't see—

I'm thinking of Anderson
the balloonist
       who spoke about
silence
in flight
    a dog's bark
slammed door
or wind
peeling off mountain rocks
     climbed
to his ear—
       He felt
nothing godlike
      but suddenly
utterly small

Overheated, damp,
tonight's wind roots at ivy
spilling from its pot
on the sill.

Half in a drowse,
I watch the vines dancing,
listen to leaves
rattle, halt—then
shake again,
as if to tear loose and scatter
through my room,
the walls dim, uncertain.

Outside, the streetlamp's drifting
among blown maples—
I brood
on their patched quilt of shadows,

 remembering someone who insisted
the dead you love come back
in sleep, telling me
a dream twice: how
with her mother and father
she laughed, joined a holiday throng,
and woke happy, assured
of peace—

The door, I think she said,
is always open. If you
go to meet them, let them through.

For Lorine Niedecker in Heaven

Lorine, Lorine
the catch is
in—

      fish scales
crystal en-
crusted among the
wet grasses

House roof's
new-shingled
now, the walls
done all in
white—
      Nothing for
you but to
drift the river:
"a silent boat"
in this hollow of
green, leaf-shady
& still

But see, a visitor,
the sun has
come, dropping through
birches & firs—
        its light
spreads a band
on your hair,
      Lorine
the catch is in

For James Wright From a Dream, 1978

I

"How do you know it's right?"
you ask, sitting
heavy-shouldered, while I
praise one of your poems
in a dream.
            I'm sure,
and say so. We
talk on over coffee
of how the moon
rising
leaves a track to shimmer
along the Loire—
you trill the *r* like music—
its long finger of light
reaching beneath
the arch of each stone bridge.

We speak too
about your beloved Max Jacob,
who saw the Lord in visions on his wall.
Strangely, you tell
of reading him at the Chicago Public Library:
"They had two volumes,
in French—"

            Then my dream,
spun out, dissolves . . .

II

I think of you
at nightfall
gazing into currents of New York traffic—

But it's the Loire, or the black Ohio
where our bones go, and only a single
blue or white wing
lifts aloft
to sail into the trees, banked wildflowers,
and tall grass burning green
across the iron water
ruined lives lie down in and sleep.

Returns

Days of fog
at the lake's edge—
           smoky white
in clouds blown down
over houses
               tatters
snagged in the leafing
elms
       & the sun
a colorless disk
that tries to burn through

Crabapple tree & cherry
have blossomed
                 then shed
in a blizzard of petals
         the recalcitrant
ailanthus
             presses tight
             ruddy spikes
from each branch—

               Year after
year seeing them
slowly
go green
           above a backyard
brick wall
where sparrows gather to
chatter
           in a dream of
stems reaching
of lengthening grass
                   that always
returns   like gulls up-
river & back
to shore
           or light on my sill
after rain passes

III

FOR A DAY

—for my mother

The weight

> —after Philippe Jaccotet

the weight of
stones
   & also
my thoughts

"i" dream—
but there are
mountains outside

nothing will
balance
   we've
lived in a
different world / some-
where between

End of December

I

end of
December—
        one gull
pulls through grey air
the mist low
over inland water
           & swings down
a wide empty arc

      wind-
snagged like these
peeling birches
         I lean in
among them, face
to the sleet, the bone tooth
of cold

II

some nights, here or
there, the sky
opens—
      so clear
the dipper's icy ladle
thick peel of
moon dropping west—

         under its
vanishing light
      rows of black
trees're pitched to a
gale's whine/
        the grasses & bare
        weeds flow
submissively

Cover

        snow cover
the first this
winter
            ice thatching
bushes, raw glaze on the
elm stumps/
                    nineteen
years ago
now
        that day the ground was too
frozen to dig
                    —and in July a
            white stone
flat with the grass

1/31

I

January's last sun
            in its
declension/
        a white blur
through clouds stretched
flat
   like sheets of worn
scrubbed muslin—

         but escapes
         now
into view:
        florescence of
orange pink crimson
dyeing chimneys
         walls
the forked sticks
         trees
         thrust up
out of their crowns
         & the firm
trunks plumbing
snow

II

after this winter's
one blizzard
        a week-
long thaw:
        southerly gusts
driving the sky clear
          put a shine
          on things—
the whips of forsythia
          greenish & grey
so wetly glimmering
          & the rivers down
          in gutters
cut dazzling furrows

III

        a pause
over
standing water/
          this little pond: the
melted snow near young
locust trees
       its wind-
scudded surface
         of a sudden
goes calm
      & underneath you
see twigs, a leaf or
two
    in a bed of dulled tan grass—

      even broken
 stems
can comfort the eye, lying as
they do,
      swept back
in a kind of sleep

Mid-winter

    a damp
windless morning
                    sifts
its particles
            minute by
minute / flakes of
snow
        soaked into stone

Grey & then

               I

               Grey
& then
greyer—
        sodden ground
the air limp/
           no stir
during a night's
mist
        —& morning
still threaded
            in a net
of fine rain

               II

               Standing out
among wet
leaves
            under a plum-
tree's reach—
            now the wind's
started up
           skittish
& works around
north—

               III

               An ear
here to listen
              eye that
attends
           the swish of
an ash
branch
           green-sprigged &
full
    or moon
            bellying
as the clouds
come un-
    stuck

A Narrow Space

>   I

a late sun un-
loads
      its fires—

east & overhead
          March sky with
bands of
high
      flattened clouds
thinning to a
      rinsed-out
blue

>   II

green ivy
        fleshed
leaf of primrose
          in their
window ledge pots

      branches of newly-
planted
      maple & ash
yield
      stiff with
protest
      to the wind's
erratic charge

III

walk (you said
            & keep
to a narrow
space
        twisting rags of
        memory
into small tapers
                that flame
& die out

IV

night:
        a new season
crosses mud-
        rutted fields
west of the
            Des Plaines

in the park
        clumps of brown grass
stand up
            urged maybe by
glittering chips
of starlight
            or the moon's
blanched gaze
            as it elevates
dead & simplified
                    straight
into heaven

You Were Saying

    sycamore tips
that stir almost
furtively
        in brusque
changeable, late
March air—

       and last night's
moon
    starting to
fill itself up
again
    lit part of the
sky
  a deep feathery
blue: "like an under-
wing," you were saying
       then didn't
continue

Yard Song

Forsythias in a
yard—
          they droop
loosely
          branches en-
tangled after a night's
wind
          the leaves
weighted with
rain
          though a few
tall shoots of
brightest green
          stick up
straight
          inching
for the sky
          & pink or white spirea
flowers:
          narrow stems
against
a back wall
          where I find
          also
this fern's
          ancient shape
risen & fingering
          the damp shadowed
air
under an ailanthus

Half-way in June

    This mid-June
sundown:
        elm, locust, young
ash &
        O willow
over the park pond
            flashing in a last
surprise eyebeam
of light—
        a gift
given
        just as the sky's
bleached-out pink
            slips quickly
into faint grey—
        then darker
west: "bruise
blue"
        where rain will arrive
before morning
        & the wind
elbow through,
        gouging some clumps
from the trees in yard
or street:
        stripped off
stems, twigs
        & heaps of shiny
wet leaves
        as half-way in my fiftieth
year passes—

For a Day

> —for Felix & Selma Stefanile

I

Awake at
first grey light—
clouds, yes
& heavy
here—
a thin
rain dropping straight
into the
motionless, water-
sleeked trees/
tchip tchip tchip
of sparrows
somewhere
beyond view—

II

Enough for a
day to discover
"square-
tipped" chicory that's
sky blue/
luminous against this
drizzle
& firm on its slickening
stems
when picked
(as I tried foolishly
to do
in a wet
lot full of
weeds—

For John Perlman

such a
slow
clouding
up

the day's
blue
brilliance
muted

faintly
at first
then wind
snaps

along the
river
tight
white-edged

waves
roughening
its
surface

gulls
swerve over
& don't
dive

June rains

June rains come
                    abruptly
spattering ledge & slant
roof, the raised window frames—

                    a refined music too
among the leaves we
walk under
                    & small
ponds standing in grass—

          this billowing of
bodies flinging loose
tresses/
          no: ash limbs've
given in &
                they
    sway—

Was it

I

Was it
spiderwort, bluet or
blue-eyed grass/
　　　　　there, inside a narrow
yard—
　　　& I paused, nearly in
secret
　　　to look—

II

To walk again
　　　　　　& to find
under my feet
　　　　　white
tops of
clover,
　　　the park's cut grass
stuck wet
to both shoes—

　　　　　Reaching down then,
brush off the leather/
　　　　　　　leaving
　　　　　　　on palm
& fingers
　　　the thin distinct blades,
each one
　　　un-
faded

78

III

      Gone—
this word itself
           hollowed
at the center/
         & so these faces
float into an afternoon's
half-sleep:
        grandfather
father   & others/
          printed briefly
their features like shadows of
cloud
     on Red Cedar river, on the
Des Plaines
       sliding along
a watery skin
         downstream &
gone—

7/16

   I

such stillness:
   humid air's dense
here/a blur
   & won't shake free even a
branch end of fluttery
plum or
   pry one nod from the
blossom-topped spirea

   II

  leaf/
   leaves
begonia, jade, english
ivy
  —each cool to my
  touch
though faced
   straight into after-
noon sun
blistering the sill

   III

   night
heat/a half
sleep under the fan's
low metal drumming—

wilted sheets, soaked
pillow
  & a figure slides by
as I seem to grasp for
shoulders, then
   head,
my lips brushing
nothing but a
   space stirred, thin
wake of your
passage
  shaping again into walls,
floor, chair &
   window: the un-
wanted dawn—

Pieces of August

I

A quick damp
summer—
         this morning
the sky's
         early white goes
grey
      hazed-
over
      layered with
drifting smoke
         & the makings
of rain—

II

         Green berries
show up
       hard as dried
peas
     bunched among the
     ivy
its leaf-
shade
      darkening even more
the wall's
brick & stone

III

After dusk—
        sibilance of tires
on wet
concrete
      rain steady
against roof slates
          then the drains
over-
flow

81

IV

       Big yellow
cat's eye
        out of
blackness—
        it's a
streetlamp
        staring through
the maples' dance:

        branches
a-
stray
      so they dip
rise
   & part way
   turn
in the square of
my unlit
      window—

Only Air

Fading rose
chalk
          a washed-
          out blue
dusk settles
the late August sky

Shadows well up
in pools
          a cicada
strikes belly music
          metallic
          against the dark

Are you there
& we talk of stars
          of a moon
          dropping
thin swatches of light

I could touch a sleeve
or hand—
          but there's time
          the clouds
haven't moved one
inch
       this moon's
       stationary as a
portrait   flushed & brilliant

The stars pulse & pulse

Who's breathing   You are
only air—
          I'm staring
          into darkness
& can't hear
the cicada

A small wind   smoke-drift
voices
down the street
                    An ailanthus
                    branch
scrapes my cheek
               as if I'd been
falling to sleep

Follow that

  follow that
roof's pitch,
              sharp
line of gutter,
drain—
        then up, back &
beyond to
           daylight de-
scending
         so the west's
nearly not
         blue, nor grey
either/
        there's a
whitish
        hue to it
        though
going dark ever
faster
        —think now
now mica bright those
sidewalks
         where the sun
was—

Out early

out early in
fog
     light drizzle

shoulders humbled to
                         rake up/shovel &
                         bag leaves
packed ankle high
on back steps, at a fence

                    the street's spine
shining
        arches wet black
behind it
            & drifted inland a little
this pair of coasting
               lake gulls
        airy
   over me

9/81

              I

For a short
while
        is all
this mid-
September
                sun's
rusty orange
                coats angled
roof & ledge/
                fades down
a west wall
          trapped by
vines—

              II

            Let
drift—
          end of a
thread
          & held to
the air's
least pull/
            you're
            cloudlike
or as haze
          over the
water
          but
"easy enough to see
through"
                —and look:
there are
leaves now
            & then maybe
            a star
or two—

86

In a Bar, Santa Fe

> —for Dave Etter

Through smoke
curling
over milk &
bourbon
      the color
of cocoa
in its sweating
glass
      she turned to
her friend—
      "When I
brought them
home, my daughter
says: These flowers
remind me of
      death
they're so hot &
droopy—"

11/17

     Rain-sopped
brown maple & the big leaves
  hand's width
           limp on sycamores

I count up nail
heads
     dulled silver in a fence's
wet slats
      still alert for
a wind pulling out of the Dakotas
              for the quick
dry
  bite of sleet

Song

       one branch
—no, almost a
dozen
       the knotted &
splay twigs
          come clear
in the window
           leafing or
as now
       un-
leaved
       with a few
finger-length tips
          scarlet
under cold November's
sun
    & this "sky full of islands"
you said:
          clouds
broken & afloat
          in blue
"o utterly blue" air
            while below
the tree's spiked
          shadow leans across grass-
          stalks
stiff with frost—

For the New Year

I

A day's
light snow, almost
like wind-flung
pollen—
    & my hand
testing the shreds of
December leaf,
      or eye
turned most
closely,
    intent on
a black-spotted birch
  —"lenticels,"
where the bark's worked
loose in
tattered bands

II

Long-
stemmed roses
on the table,
    sent by a
friend,
& white too: "for the
new year"
    —as if one
started once again—
    this frigid air
in bursts, bringing
ice to a high
shine,
    tunneling or
resurfacing drifts

IV

RECENT POEMS

Lit

       I

     then with March
             beginning
with greyish,
       soot-
specked snow: thin cover on
ledge, fence post & porch
rail/
     a stump's raw
gleam of elm-
       flesh exposed &
brighter than ice under
the clouds—

       II

      lean, its
branches all up-
reaching,
      the cherry tree's
so close
     & shudders from lake wind/waves
lathering a
      broken
stone pier, heaped
pilings
       —no one's out
here in these gusts but dozens of
gulls flock on shore/
        this afternoon
such as it is
      lit by white curves
of their necks
& backs—

Early sun's

          early sun's
up, catching at
                    thistles—
blur of
yellow rounding them
                    darkens the purple
heads on their
                    tall
spiny stalks—

                    in my
dream last night
                    was arrival/some
place come to,
                    achieved—
now even thought of it's
gone,
          all but
a trace—
          like this morning's half
moon: faint
chalkmark arc
                    powdered
into the blue—

                    light's every-
where/flashing off the blades & small
teeth
          of leaves

Wrapped

      one long
branch crooked
up:
          an elbow/
                    this locust
in wind, its whole
frame giving
              a little—
September's heat
at eighty or
more
        & damp

   mostly in
shade,
          weeding
down among &
                  under impatiens,
ginger, these scarce
ferns
        turning a dry brown

        leaves
loosening, the clouds
above
        bundled together:
first bright, then
grey, wavelike
                  pass across high
flat rooftops
to lose themselves

            my fingers prod into
wet dirt/stiff with
                    their grappling
        wrapped
around roots—

No Clouds

I

        No clouds here
not one—
           full sun drenches
the porch rail
           where blowflies
           glint blue
in a stupor of warmth
& brilliance—
           though small gusts
cool from the lake
             flick my window-
shade out & back
             against the wood
frame   the single-paned glass
raised up—

II

        Locusts at work
in the park
           have halted—
but the sparrows won't
quit
     & still forage
in pairs   or more—
              just now they're
suddenly ablaze
           rounded small bodies
caught by the west-falling
light—

96

III

       Shadows too
form a tight wedged
corner
     this place where
     & in which
foliage thickens—
          damp nearly un-
breathable air
taking hold
       hangs over leaf mold & dirt
—a slow sinking
      before the
sun dies—

      I

  rainless damp:
blanched, burnt-up grass,
ferns,
     a trio of maples turning
early in August's long
dog days
       & no
relief

      II

  over my frame
back porch
     a hot tumult of leaves &
"winged fruit":
       sunlight's
shaken off a "weed"
tree of heaven
      in a dazzle of
flakes, chips/
     gulf
    winds threshing it
mixed with the cicadas' high
declining
    rattle

III

   nearly fifty-
two, here
in this yard
        I finger a smooth
ginger leaf,
         needle-sharp holly
but think instead of roots: wet,
secret & cool

          —though most of a
river/
   tires hiss on a bridge
above the Des Plaines'
         brown lagging flow, then
follow a road into remembered
woods—

Three Songs

                    I

    morning wind's
southwest—
                a swift
                heat/
                        sun
running over forsythia
tips, the first
                yelloweyed
white blossoms of
    blood
    root—

            II

    a "desire to
let go"/whatever hold
you had,
            "tenuous": yes
though not like the
catkins
            which dropped
sodden off poplars
    in last night's
rain—

            III

    0
            blue:
bluet & bell
flower/
            fleur

    star,
vase or
            cup shaped—
fragile these
petals
            & the stem's
strong green—

Mornings now

Mornings now the dawn
light clarifies
slowly,
            picking out the reach of
any top branch
                  inch by
inch—
         but today's hesitant
grey rain
            blurs across leaves/
                           brittle &
quick to fall—

                     Still,
white sweet clover's
little obelisks,
               chicory in bunches
with a scattering of lavender
thistleheads
            spread through a
fenced-off lot—
               my feet stopped on the wet
walk outside—

Then

> this
lifting
> to struggle from a
dream's pull/
> its pain where someone's
been shamed, cast
out—
> there's dawn
sky now: weak
purple-hued blue
> with the
quarter moon's fine curve
still visible/
> cutting west through loose
slips of cirrus—
> then risen into my
body among yellowed bird-
cherry leaves, rough sycamores
> i'm unnoticeable

here like roadside
thistles in a ditch
> or a surviving
fern's green stem

A first freeze

I

          A first freeze
brings down
                    ailanthus stems,
long tough ones/
                    thick,
slippery beneath my
heel
          & wind-
swept to the flowerbed's
edge—

II

          Sky, ground,
lake—
          each a
different grey/
                    tree
roots, bushes packed in
fine snow,
                    the white lines of
house tops
                    holding
their own,
                    this moment
of your moments—
                    "You were
standing here
                    & then you
were not—"

Sun's along

    sun's along this
wall early—
            holly, limp ginger
try on a small
gloss/
        white paint set a-
blaze: each chip, crack,
                line &
its shadow
         refined/all
for a while precise—

    wet ground too:
            these last
clumps of snow, ice
draining off—
         water flashes in
weeds, in the grass below slopes

    —slipping through stalks, un-
leaved twigs,
        i'm only a little less
transparent than the
            lighted
air—

Ailanthus, yes

      ailanthus, yes—
& this window square
blocked in grey /
               unruly branches
jab their hooked tips
         at rain glazing them
changing now back to
snow—

      not any dream, what
she told me /
         of having "lived
long enough—
        it's just how
to know where
you're going—"

      even under clouds
the wind
dropping,
       small banks, drifts
       get lit/faintly
blue at dark &
        piled toward my yard's
south margin,
      its row of
reddish boards
        shoulder to shoulder with
cold-stiffened forsythia
leaning down—

I

      Almost no
winter: early
heat
    and now March gets
a start—
      this faint
gloss
    as of
something rubbed
rounds out
      an undersize plum
tree
    the ash
branches and trunk—

II

      Last week
walking beside
me
    alive in a dream
you fell
suddenly down
      and were gone
again
    as I groped for
you, woke
      these spoon-shapes of a
jade plant
     had leaned to
take light
on the sill—

Two Views

I

    April
birches & maples /
        bare
saplings
    all of them
    spindly-limbed
rock a little
    under the north wind's
steady spring pounding /
       these few young
cedars the only green
in a view
    rain-
soaked grey & brown

II

    no storm in
this picture /
     tracks
laid on wood
trestles
    rise over miles of
marsh land
    east &
oblique to a sun
     climbing hot
from dawn haze /
     grass
steaming in clumps & dead
trees—

    each step's
measured
    tie to
tie/not to slip
through
    always an ear for
a far-off whistle
    feet tense at the
slightest vibration
of rails—

Listened for

   listened for—
a cardinal's
"slurred" whistle in the
rain
  his red crest its
flicker amidst
     the pale green
glistening of
    just
budded leaves
    /
     criss
crossed the black wires
       humming with
voices above &
     beneath them from
each jonquil's burst
petals
   a yellow
  corona—

        —for Theodore Enslin

      skin of
mist over slates, rails, stone
ledges
      /
      wind-turned
the leaves provide a
damp sheen on
           either side in what
light's here—
       not "viri-
descence" but these maples' deepest
green
      going grey at dusk now
almost black where
each branch
        reaches from its trunk
& tonight's huge
         shadow-
less moon
      /out of sight
whitens only the
tops of clouds

Cat/eyes

        —for James Weil

      cat
eyes a
      ladybug's
slow
motions
      the opposite
side of this window screen

            /stand-off
where thin woven
         wire
  inter
     venes

          sparrows, robins
                              still
talkative near
dusk /
          tree to
tree
     & under a thin cloud
layer
          violet
streaked on grey

     at street's end
a park:
              grass sloping down this
hollow
          aged high
oaks over
               hang / deep shadowed
beneath
                         —here a daughter
tall now
as i
     with small hands &
body once made
                         snow angels / wings
fanning as they rose
                         sun
                         lit & hidden in
 air a whirl of
               chipped
                         crystal—

Yellowish grass-

      yellowish grass-
glitter after rain
               & leaves drying
in an otherwise subdued
light—

         time to gather up
sprigs, stems,
           wind-hacked
branches /
        whatever the
storm flung down—
            but this
lacy fern's not hurt,
          the pink-
steepled spirea
         hold their sway—

    i'd stay here with the air
barely weighing on
            clusters of ginger
or stirred in a
breath that
       comes &
goes over ground where early
                 wild
blue violets grew—

First to

    first to
fall/
       this litter of fruit
                          crab-
apple & cherry leaves
                    under sky such a tight
whitened blue /
          crow
          call thinning out
north over the
beeches   a row of new willows
shaking free

        "when the
       wind changes—"
                          i
     remember
                acorns hammered
my grandmother's roof
               rolled into
drifts in its tarred
corners
     /
      summer ending then &
now only
     "a life
  ago"

10/31

    —nothing,
                     a
leaf / blown among
                      others
to the ridged
           stone
stoop

In clear sunlight &

in clear sunlight & there's
a wind honed so
things glisten / branch
shadows
which move by the inch
across fine
dry snow a
few knots of grass thrust
up through
with bluish grey
shade over the yard's
brittle ice

now

one
flung oblong of
brightness
falls
into a
room
& out past table &
window pane
these smallest
cherry shoots
standing quite bare
lighted as they curve
sky
ward   or
rise on the
diagonal
while from some
where not far
sparrows' unflagging
chatter possesses my
ear /
no /
the whole air

115

Acknowledgements

Grateful acknowledgement is made to editors and presses for poems which appeared in the following limited edition collections: *Night Road/Poems* (Ernest Stefanik, The Rook Press); *With No Answer* (John Judson, Juniper Press); *March Light* (Felix Stefanile, Sparrow Press); *For a Day* (David Pichaske, Spoon River Poetry Press).

Further acknowledgement is due to the editors of periodicals in which many of these poems appeared, sometimes in different form: *A: a Journal of Modern Literature; Another Chicago Magazine; Ascent; Centennial Review; Cottonwood Review; Dacotah Territory; Descant; Longhouse; The Madison Review; The Menomonie Review; Mississippi Valley Review; Moons and Lion Tailes; New England Review; New Jersey Poetry Journal; New Letters; New Mexico Humanities Review; Northeast; Poem; Spoon River Quarterly; Tar River Poetry; Telescope; Uzzano.*

"Brief Thaw" also appeared in *Prairie Voices*, edited by Lucien Stryk (Illinois Arts Council Foundation/Spoon River Poetry Press); "Yellow" and "Beeches" in *Banyan Anthology 2*, edited by Mary Trimble, Richard Sanford, Hymie Luden, and Barry Silesky (Banyan Press); "A Fall Song" in *Anniversary Note: Sparrow 1954-1984*, edited by Felix and Selma Stefanile (Sparrow Press).

"Mid-August," "Two Poems," and "Song" received Illinois Arts Council Awards for Poetry; *March Light* the Carl Sandburg Prize for poetry, Friends of the Chicago Public Library.

Thanks to Michael Anania, Jim Elledge, Theodore Enslin, David Ignatow, August Kleinzahler, David Pichaske, Felix Stefanile, Lucien Stryk, and James Weil for various kinds of help and support.

R.J.M., Jr.